YOUR WORLD

YOUR FAMILY

Michael Pollard

Wayland

Your World

Your Community
Your Family
Your Friends
Yourself

First published in 1989 by
Wayland (Publishers) Limited
61 Western Road, Hove
East Sussex, BN3 1JD, England

Series Editor: Mike Hirst
Series Designer: Sally Boothroyd

British Library Cataloguing in Publication Data
Pollard, Michael, *1931 –*
    Your family.
    1. Families. – For children
    I. Title II. Series
    306.8'5

ISBN 1 85210 760 X

Typeset by Lizzie George, Wayland
Printed and bound by Casterman, S.A., Belgium

Contents

All the words that appear in
bold are explained in the
glossary on page 22.

You are part of your family.

Your family is a group of **special** people. You may have a mother, father, brothers, sisters, grandparents, aunts and uncles. They are all part of your family.

Families often have a meal together.

Some of them may live with you in your home. Others may live somewhere else. All the people in your family are your **relatives**.

*Some people live in **extended families.***

Every family is different.

Your family is different from any other family. Some families are very large. Other families are quite small.

There are two brothers and one sister in this family.

You may see one of your parents more than the other.

A mother or a father in a family is called a **parent**. You may have just one parent. Or you may live some of the time with one parent, but visit your other parent at weekends or holidays. Some children live with **foster parents** or in a children's home.

Families often like to meet together.

People in families like to talk and joke.

Relatives sometimes visit each other even if they live in different places. They can come together at **weekends**, or at special times like birthdays.

*You can learn
how to do
things from your
family.*

It is fun to join in and do things
with other people in your family.
Doing things together helps you
to get to know your family better.

You know your family better than you know anyone else.

You spend more time at home than anywhere else. You see members of your family when they are sad or angry as well as when they are feeling happy and cheerful.

Your family can help you when you are upset.

Families like to meet when it is someone's birthday.

People who live together learn to understand and help each other in bad times as well as good times.

In a happy family, people help each other.

People in a family share the work that has to be done at home.

Washing the dishes is one way of helping.

You feel safe when someone loves you.

Older members of a family help to look after the younger ones. People in a family like helping the others because they love them.

People in families make each other happy.

When we love people, we like to show it. We like to make the people we love feel happy. There are many ways of showing our love for people in our family.

We like to talk and listen to people we love.

We like to give them hugs and kisses. Sometimes we give them presents too. Giving things makes us happy.

Breakfast in bed is a treat for mum and dad.

Someone in your family has time to listen to you.

Someone in your family can help if you have a problem.

If you are scared or unhappy you need to talk to someone about it. People in your family can listen to you and help you.

Sometimes it is your turn to listen to someone else. Things do not seem so sad or **frightening** when you can tell someone in your family about them.

You can tell someone in your family if you are unhappy.

Even in families, people do not agree all of the time.

People in families sometimes **quarrel**. They may argue about important things, or about something that is not very serious at all.

People in families sometimes argue.

If you argue with someone it does not mean that you have stopped loving each other. When you have finished arguing, you can be as loving as you were before. Making up again is important. It helps families to feel safe and happy together.

You can make friends again after a quarrel.

If your mother has a new baby, your family will have another member.

Babies need to learn to love and trust their family. Sometimes parents may **adopt** a new member of the family too.

Everyone can help when there is a new baby.

People in families are good friends.

We should show that we love all new members of the family by talking to them, smiling and playing with them. It is important for all the people in a family to love and care for each other.

21

Glossary

Adopt　　　　　To bring into your family someone who does not have a family of their own.

Extended family　A big family where lots of different relatives live together.

Foster parents　Foster parents look after children who cannot live with their own family.

Frightening　　Making you scared.

Parent　　　　A mother or a father.

Presents　　　Things you give to other people.

Quarrel　　　Argue angrily.

Relatives　　　People who are members of the same family.

Special　　　Important.

Weekends　　Saturdays and Sundays.

Books to read

Children Need Families   Michael Pollard
  (Wayland, 1988)
Family Life   B. McConville (Macdonald, 1988)
My Family   Kati Teague (Macdonald, 1988)

Picture acknowledgements

Chapel Studios 5, 7, 8, 10, 17; Sally and Richard Greenhill *cover*, 11, 14, 20; Wayland Picture Library 4, 6, 15, 16, 18, 19; Timothy Woodcock Photolibrary 9, 12, 13, 21.

Index